THIS IS NOT ABOUT LOVE: POEMS

KRYSTAL A. SMITH

THIS IS NOT ABOUT LOVE: POEMS

KRYSTAL A. SMITH

Published by BLF Press
Clayton | Bloomington

This is Not About Love: Poems © 2021 by Krystal A. Smith All rights reserved. No part of this publication may be reproduced, distributed, or transmitted in any form or by any means, including photocopying, recording, or other electronic or mechanical methods, without the prior written permission of the publisher, except in the case of brief quotations embodied in critical reviews and certain other noncommercial uses permitted by copyright law. For permission requests, contact the publisher.

Printed in the United States of America

First Printing, 2021

Cover Art: Efe Kurnaz
Cover Design: Lauren Curry

ISBN Print: 978-1-7359065-2-2

"Cycles" first appeared online at *Entropy Magazine* January 2020

"Extinction" first appeared online at *Kissing Dynamite* March 2020

"Ode to Joy" first appeared as "Discovering Joy" in *Mental Realness Mag* both in print and online September 2020.

Table of Contents

9   Easement

10   Cycles

11   Coming Back to Silence

12   I. When the White Women in the Office Start to Whisper

13   Not the Loneliness I Had Planned For

14   Bend Back the Days

15   Say it With Me

16   Sangria

17   Wishbone

18   Extinction

19	365
20	Body of Knowledge
21	Reaching Out
22	Forgiveness (Middle of the Night Poem)
23	Proximity
24	Mama Said
25	Mise En Place
26	II. When the White Women in the Office Start to Whisper
27	Explore the Deep
28	Antecedents
29	Regarding the Climax Occurring 34 Degrees 14 Minutes 3 Seconds N., 77 Degrees 49 Minutes 36 Seconds W.
30	Thick
31	Retaining, Recovering

32	Paradise is Loving You Alcorn, Mississippi
33	The Crooked Line of Your Mouth
34	If You Scared, Say You Scared
35	The New Woman
36	III. When the White Women in the Office Start to Whisper
37	To Be Chosen, To Choose
38	Ode to Joy
39	Fragments & Light
41	Acknowledgements
43	About the Author

Easement

What settles in my hand
I let settle in my hand
no gripping, no grabbing
no presumption it will stay
adjust &
be easy;
balanced
flutter, then rock
steady, and sway
upward float, gentle
each day (each day)
what settles in my hand
I let settle in my hand

Cycles

Water from the last storm

has finally gone, receded

into earth.

The rings of its visit

show on the side

of the house. You were

that tall once, measured

in string and charcoal

by Papa's hands. He moved

like water, like rain. Steady,

steady,

then slow until

not at all.

Memories move like that

too. There, then not there.

Coming Back To Silence

Let me slip
        into death
                like a canoe noses
                        into water at dawn
                              Let Flowers trail behind
                                      to signal nature I'm coming back home
                                                Let the birds sing
                                                        and the wind

Let the desire to speak be drowned out by
                                          clapping, crashing waves
                                    keep quiet
                                        Let silence ring
                                                Let silence ring
                                                    Let silence
                                                        be a eulogy

.

I.
When the White Women in the Office Start to Whisper

I cringe.

I keep working.

I try to ignore them,
I strain to hear,
I distract myself.

I make myself small.
I ready myself.

Not the Loneliness I Had Planned For

My loneliness is caked with grief, heavy, and sagging.
It's come much too soon, all at once.
I'm older than my years, but not ready to stop pretending.

This loneliness is not at all what I'd planned for.

> Where are the quiet sunny days bathed in charming solitude?
> Do I ever learn to garden? Nurture useful beauty from the ground?
> Chase the dog out of my tomatoes?

There is too much space, so much distance and disaster, crushing.
What I find myself with is blurry and burned.

The dog is dead.

I'm not yet forty.

Bend Back the Days

Bend back the days. Invert the sky,
place me above your heart, swear that what you feel for me is more,
more, more than you've ever known. Sing to me from far away
Sometime

Bend back the days. Fill me up until I'm the ocean,
rock me in your arms every time
we meet. Make me over.
Sometime

Bend back the days. Twist at & snatch the wind. Move slower
Let me write in your palm, press my finger over
your lifeline (pulse). My name is an incantation, a spell that
wears off in the night. Breaks.
Sometime

Bend back the days. Fold in some sun, sprinkle me along the seams.
Pack it all down into a small neat square.
Slip me in your pocket like a tune in your head.
Sometime

Say it With Me

I don't need a reason to save you
'cos I'm not saving you.

You're never concerned until it concerns you,
ain't that right, baby?

I'm taking up space for once.
You hear me?

I'm taking the space I need.
You should too.

I have survived this mess
again. Again.

You can go. Now
go.

Sangria

I hope while
you're in Spain enjoying
the local women and cuisine
you choke

on a piece
of fruit

(pineapple was always your favorite)

just long enough to get dizzy,
to get a bit closer
to God;

long enough
for you to see
me

in your mind

and when Valentine, the server,
administers the Heimlich
may you bruise like just dropped
peaches.

Wishbone

When you used to yell at me,
call me stupid and ungrateful,
I saw little pieces of your love
floating away on every angry breath.

Your boney fingers shaking
so close to my face
I thought you would ram
them straight through my skull.

Each time you called me
stupid, dummy, idiot,
I wished instead that you
would have slapped me,
or pushed me to the floor,
or twisted my arm
until my bone broke;

shattered, splintered
away from the muscle.

Extinction

My mother was your mother,
your father was my father,
but like a bad word on my name a knife cut the bloodline,
your face out of old photographs.
If I don't speak of you,
think of you,
you'll be gone.
Forgotten.

Men go extinct, brother
because they trample earth, women, with no consequence.
Taking and taking, calling it survival
until
all that's left
is the falling sky.

365

I think about how long it's been since I've heard your voice. We both exist in the same time and space (though the space you occupy is inside me).
I haven't heard your voice in over a year.
365+ days without your laugh feels wrong.

I see you peripherally, but when I turn you disappear like the reason I walked into the other room. I'm standing, trying to remember.

I'm trying to remember: You kissed my nose and stroked the scar between my eyes with your finger. I believe you reside there in the pucker.

A year is long enough
to vaguely remember,
to forget,
to give up.

A year is long enough
to want to kiss someone new.

Body of Knowledge

Your entire body lies
trembling before the touch.

Trembling before the touch
and so afraid of revealing yourself.

So afraid of revealing
who you are.

Who are you?
Have you grown? How do you know?

Oh, how you've had to grow. I know
it hasn't been easy.

No, it hasn't been easy
protecting yourself.

To protect yourself
your entire body lies.

Reaching Out

Even though you say
we're friends
and that you miss me, you miss us,

it feels inappropriate,

    muddled & messy,

to reach out to you.

I want to make you laugh
and ask after the fellas.

    But I keep my words to myself.

Until it all spills out
onto some page
I can't erase.

I loved you again today.

Forgiveness
(Middle of the night poem)

Forgiveness is not a weapon
it is a learning, it is a lesson
to give to yourself

It is a moment to let go,
a moment to care

It is a chance to dare
to grow

Like the tallest trees
steady in the ground, roots
deep but limbs free to reach
for the next bit of air

To breathe again.

Proximity

In my dreams we glide
into one another and glisten.
Amoeba-like, transferring energy,
knowledge and such, back and forth.
We embrace—
One one-thousandth, two.

I learn
for the next attachment;
skin on skin, shallow breaths.

Proximity made us lovers.

Mama Said

Stop crying before I give you something to cry about.
She gave and gave and gave.
She gave me everything she had.

Mise en Place

Regardez
everything in its place
parce que everything has a place

You & me
is a place
You inside me
(vous en moi)
A new dimension

My place
is here
(ici, ici)
I know now
your distance
is non/desire

I'm here
(Je suis là)

I was not prepared,
(Je n'étais pas préparé)

only put away

Mise en place
but misplaced
(mais égaré)
put in my place
(Mettre à ma place)

II.
When the White Women in the Office Start to Whisper

It's followed by siren shrill
laughs that linger,
that fill up space so violently
the black on my back welts.

Explore The Deep

We explore the deep
bent knees
to chest

Breath

c l o u d i n g over
collarbone,
hips grinding
bone

Searching for
the knot
the head
the tip

the wet earth
rising
fragrant

We are painted
on each other now

Stained

Antecedents
[an(t)ə'sēdnt]

Ann -- the first woman you love who doesn't love you back. Or maybe she does but doesn't know how to show it. She's too busy keeping you alive. Mothering. She does the best she knows how but it often hurts. You fix your face, your attitude, your tone and certainly do not give her a reason to give you something to cry about. You're afraid of her. But she's still the most beautiful woman you've ever seen.

Anna -- from work is still rightfully angry about being molested by her cousin/daddy/brother but swears Bill Cosby told the truth and that those women were lying. She yells it at you. The louder her voice the more direct her words will penetrate, she thinks. She doesn't know you carry the same stench and pressure, some man's dick pressed into your back and no one believing you. She just yells and quits the next day. You know hurt people hurt people.

Anne -- She is more than one person you decide after her paring knife peels away your delicate skin and she squeezes you to pulp. She slurps you up. You love every minute. She buys you trinkets, but never gives you anything real. You make excuses for her behavior, her lack of follow through.
She might as well be your mother for all the disappointment you find yourself holding. She is the first woman, after so long, who you want to love, but she doesn't love.

Regarding the Climax Occurring 34 degrees 14 minutes 3 seconds N, 77 degrees 49 minutes 36 seconds W

The rosé burst in the freezer
pink slush clumped on
smooth white plastic

My shoulder stung from
your bite
my neck jealous, my ass awaiting
I came alive beneath your teeth

I scooped with my bare hands
the soft fluff, swirled my fingers
in it 'til they were numb

You almost let me

touch my lips
to the sticky
sweet residue

You almost let me

touch you
too

Thick

The hum of bees
and the musky odor of pinks
filled the air.
I looked around for you,
slow to remember
your absence deliberate.
I was bleeding underneath
my skin.
Aching
for you,
for it,
the beginning
stretched out
like some
illusion.

I could not master
use of language
for as badly
as I wanted to
call out, say
to you
goodnight, *yes*, and *please*.
My tongue
aligned with the roof
of my mouth,
as thick
as fog

stifling, stifling.

Retaining, Recovering

No more you for me.
    (I'm done. Thank you.)
I'll want to talk to you still.
    (Maybe)
Too much back and forth.
Too much you've not made your mind up about.
So, no. No more
loose ends, no
more *be well*.
Just let me be.
Let my Black ass be.
I don't want to know
more than I have to.
    (I know too much already. I know too much.)
It's all baggage. I have
but two arms, two hands.
I want nothing on my back.
    (Get off my back)
And nothing more in my head.
Let my cells filter everything
down to particles, down
to water. (Thirsty thirties)
I'm bloated, retaining.
Recovering still from
1992
    (the first time I bled).
I'm tired. Let me be.

Paradise is Loving You
Alcorn, Mississippi

You believe in signs? I do. I do and I have ever since I was a child listening to my grandma while she fixed supper, showing me how to make things outta whatever was laying around.

Why does this book I'm reading mention a place I associate with you and only you specifically by name? When earlier I was trying my best not to think about you or call you or get you a message somehow.

This book that's been in the world long, long before our paths crossed, but I'm not reading 'til now after I met you, fell for you, got my heart snatched up and thrown back by you. That's a sign, baby. That's a sign that maybe I don't know how to read.

But I would give you another chance to be in my life
if you wanted it.

Baby, this *here* is a sign. I keep reading and rereading the lines that make me feel all warm and there you are in my mind as clear as a picture. I knew it—knew something—when I first met you. The way you hugged me and rocked me and smiled and looked me in the face.

My word.
My God.
My LOVE.

The Crooked Line of Your Mouth

Hovering
above your body—
my thighs
squeezing your thigh—
as I ride
to oblivion.
The crooked line
of your mouth
formed by my name, Lover.
Get it.
Get it all.

If You Scared, Say You Scared

I like how the old heads talk
loud, boisterous.
Everything a reference
to a time before now. They say, "What
you know about that right there? Huh?"
Everything is a riddle.
They'll make fun of you,
but let you in a little, let you in on the joke.
Because everything is
a joke.
It's their way.
It's our way.
Because we are a people
of joy and making it through
whatever. The laughter keeps you
well. Even when it's not all good we joke.

Bravado in our voices, "Shiid, if you
scared, say you scared." But we never
do say.

The New Woman

A new lover is here. She
says, "How I've prayed
for a woman like you." She
says, "You are my joy." She
says, "Forever." She
does not hear me unzipping
my skin at night, opening
myself wide, and packing
my limbs and torso with clumps
of wet black dirt. The worms
are buried deep, they wrap around
the bone, snacking on what
soft meat is left.

III.
When the White Women in the Office Start to Whisper

I laugh.

Then I shout,
"I can fucking hear you.

We have an open
floor plan."

Everything they do is
performative!

To Be Chosen, To Choose

I cannot wait
for you to rise
from the foaming
sea and choose
me. I cannot wait
against the sky
clinging where
clouds form, ready
for you to be ready
to want me. I will
not wade into my own
undoing for you.

I have chosen.

Ode to Joy

I laugh myself relaxed.

Consider mania
but this is no

episode.

I am present—

boundaries set,
surrounded by true
nurturing:

Friends who
have become
family;
access to more
than before,
access
to more of myself.

I exist wholly,

holy,

for me.

Fragments & Light

I stretch across the ground like a cloud.
The reflection of my body shimmers in the puddles
of water at our feet. I am here now in this moment
r i p p l i n g & e x p a n d i n g into everything. This is how you'll
remember me. I'm sure of it. Captured in fragments and light.
The bright blue sky pulls at us, making us taller than we are, more beautiful,
more capable of holding a peaceful silence inside amidst all the turmoil.
You say how you feel to the air, the trees, but never to me. I already know.
I pierce through the fog of your mind on cold windless days.

Acknowledgements

I would like to thank the Black Lesbian Literary Collective and its members who are always so willing to read and nurture my words. JHall thank you for always being ready with a positive word or two or three. My spirit is grateful for you. Sounds of Blackness forever. Stephanie thank you for creating such a welcoming Black space and inviting me in and believing in my work.

About the Author

Krystal A. Smith is a Black lesbian writer of poetry and speculative fiction. Her poetry can be read at *Entropy Magazine*, *Kissing Dynamite*, *Emerge Literary Journal*, and *Serendipity Literary Magazine*. Her debut collection *Two Moons: Stories* was released from BLF Press (2018) and was a 2019 Lambda Literary Award Finalist. She is the founder and editrix in chief of poetry journal *Inkwell Black*.

www.ingramcontent.com/pod-product-compliance
Lightning Source LLC
Chambersburg PA
CBHW081510080526
44589CB00017B/2724